IN LIEU OF FLOWERS

IN LIEU OF FLOWERS

RACHEL L. SLOTNICK

TORTOISE BOOKS

CHICAGO, IL

Dear Fisherman

A Defense of the Father
In 25 Lullabies

1. Without you there would be too many trout and the bears would grow fat and become men.

2. Yes, the greatest of your loves was mayonnaise, and you put it on everything. I ate raw catfish in a storm and paused. Between rain sounds I heard animals mewing.

3. And that was when I sank to the ocean floor. My hair turned green and followed my limbs like mermaid hair, and I complained: *All these marching starfish, ugly underwater suns.*

4. For I have stabbed your sea. For I am queen of the fish and you are nothing but a postage stamp flapping across the ocean.

5. You have a wooden stump for an arm. You fell in love with the shark and let her kiss you.

6. That's how I discovered you were really just a lonely human.

7. And then there was that time in Tiburon when you wouldn't stop singing. Your voice cracked on high notes in the traffic.

8. You cleared your throat and the sound killed a nearby bird. It fell from the sky and you jumped a little at the thud. Then your sneeze kicked a wandering dog.

9. For I would more expect a sea bird than a dove.

10. Than an old synonym for father to deliver peace in an overnight package.

11. The fact that the sequins in your eyes looked like the sequins in my dress meant nothing.

12. Your lungs are grasping tentacles and they beat while your heart breathes.

13. You forgot the names of your brothers. You looked at your mother and felt nothing.

14. And now you're still wheezing.

15. Without you, there would be too much sky. Bears and Alaskan deer would roam the subway looking out the windows.

17. Yes, the greatest kindness is cooking. How else do you tell someone you love?

18. I saw your worms after the storm and I wasn't even sad. I watched their lonely bodies and worried about my electrical bill.

19. Between lightning strikes there were more animals mewing.

20. You had an achy knee, and a metallic hip. I sailed to the horizon, searching for a cure.

21. I have made a brew of your coughs so that when you are gone, I will still have the sounds you made right before you left.

22. For you remind me of a bird hurled over a cliff, except you always forget your wings.

23. Like a cherry tree too late.

24. So I bought you an airplane.

25. And when it never crashed you looked at me through cloudy eyes, and said: *But Sweets, I'm afraid to fly.*

Tales from my Fisherman Father

In Tiburon on a Wednesday, I saw a seabird with my father's face.

"Why don't you get yourself a decent boyfriend?" it cawed.

It spiraled up and vanished, casting a flicker on the sand by my feet, like the limb of a tree breathing out slowly.

*

That night, I dreamt that my father was eaten by a bear. It swallowed him whole, like a shot of Slivovitz, and expressed disgust at the aftertaste. The bear's belly bulged, and his chin sprouted a long, tangled beard. When the bear began to hoard flashlights and parked himself in front of old Star Wars reruns on the Sci-Fi Channel, I grew suspicious. When the bear began to snore with all the rhythm and force of the ocean, I realized there was salvation in hibernation.

*

When I turned seven, my father's beard filled with salmon and seaweed. His cod eyes darted from reef to reef. He spoke in an enormous gurgling noise which made everything sound underwater. This was his lullaby. It was the sort of burbling tonality I needed in order to believe in things like that stuff that shifts the clouds.

*

When my father was a child, a shark bit off his arm. He replaced it with a wooden stump.

Naturally, he became a shark hunter, and he hated all trees for daring to resemble him. Stumps were the worst of the trees, because they were already dead.

*

My father was tormented by winter fish. He saw them everywhere: dangling from the trees, hanging in the air like reflective lures, swallowing the sky and hiccupping green ocean. I tried to explain to him that they were only apples. "See, they're not fish at all," I said as I plucked a red, ripe one, but his scaly skin tautened, and so, like he had taught me so many times, I threw it back. I watched it fall like an unanswered plea until at last, the apple hit the ocean.

*

"*My skeleton is shivering,*" he said to me once, when his thoughts turned to winter.

*

One Passover, I brought home a handsome, rich, fish of a boyfriend.

"*Is he Jewish?*" asked my father, clutching the neighborhood in the palm of his hand.

*

Once, in the hospital, my father ate an octopus. As he chomped, his eyes rolled back like a hungry predator. I watched all the legs and legs and legs.

I remember he had looked like an octopus, all those
tubes growing from his arms. I had never felt my
fingers so concretely, so many unnecessary digits.
That was when I first noticed it, supple and
strange, a perfect tentacle sprouting from the
heart of my palm.

*"If you follow your hands, you can shake the winter
fish from the trees,"* he said.

*

There we stood, just two humans looking out the
hospital window, at the edges of the fish bowl,
talking about the weather.

*

My father's stump arm flailed wildly as the train
shook. When we went underground, my father got
confused. *"Look,"* he insisted, *"There's a beautiful
glowing fish at the end of the tunnel."*

*

"We'll call him Charlie," my father said once of a
tremendous rainbow trout, as he gutted it and the
paint colors spilled out. The clouds were gray as
fish skin. My father wiped the purple blood on his
pants and said, *"Don't worry, Sweets. He's already
dead."*

*

I knew when the clocks were still in the fish skin
sky, and the carp rained down from the dying trees
like ripe apples. *"Be still,"* said my father,
fishing for forbidden fruit. The leaves hummed, and

everywhere were tentacles for hearts. I knew then
that this was the beginning of something slow.

Dear Fisherman

I collect nightcrawlers when it rains
just in case he returns from the sea.
He was always talking about Kerouac's candles
exploding like spiders across the stars.

So I look up at the night sky
in search of dorsal fins
and dissolved oxygen
that might lead me through the chum.

He told me once about catch-and-release,
and I looked back at him
and knew I had to let him go
to preserve the resource.

It's a good day for cloud cover,
he had said, brushing the dirt from his anchor.
He was referring to the cosmic clock,
and how the salmon were ripening in the trees,
unfolding their shimmering bodies
towards the lying sun.

He had looked at me then through the winter
weather,
pink as a cooked salmon,
and he had grunted something about flounders,
and fish falling from the sky.

He had looked a little like a puffer fish
blowing out his cheeks,
long-lining through the cold front.

He kept forgetting to put letters
in the bottles he kept throwing out to sea.
I continue to cast my line,
and my salmon heart breaches
every time it snags on boots from men I've
forgotten.

Human Noise (Roses)

He fell in love with the shark,
and tried to kiss her.
That was how I knew he was only a lonely human.

I watched him angling his line,
snagging for pike and mudsucker,
but he kept catching the same boot
and throwing it back.

Why he danced with the catfish,
and crossed his heart to the minnows,
I may never understand.

But some lures are better left uncast,
hibernating in the tackle box,
dreaming up at plastic stars.

Ode to Aimee Bender

When I was a child it became clear to me that my father was different from other fathers. He was gruff and unkempt, and told strange stories about the sea. He wasn't that old, but his hair was white, and his wrinkles left deep impressions in his skin, like footprints in wet sand. His eyes were two boats, casting towards the horizon.

Twenty years have passed, and it's clear now that I am losing him. My father is returning to the ocean, slowly, in the same way that we all eventually return to dust. He scratches at his beard that flaps with minnows, and when he stands in the light I can see purple and red tadpoles swimming through his veins.

When I realized my father was growing fins and gills, I wasn't upset at first. I wanted to get to know this new marine father, to understand, and smell, and swim with him, but I didn't realize my father wasn't coming back.

He told me he never meant to lose himself at sea. He just loved the chase and the storm. *"We're long-lining through the cold front,"* he would say, holding his red thumb to the wind like a flagpole to the moon. *"Its about alkalinity,"* he said, brushing algae from his anchor, *"and I'm angling for stragglers."* This had something to do with his method: isolating the weak from the pack.

I did the math. A few weeks ago he complained his heart felt heavy as a fish on the line. Last Saturday he said his tongue was slimy and thick, like an eel. At this rate, I figure we have about a month left. I took him shopping, tried to dress him up more like a man and less like an Arctic salmon. The clothes kept snagging on hooks and doorknobs. *"I'm cooked bait,"* he said, and there were marlins diving and breaching in the fog between us. Yesterday, I found him flopping in his favorite

chair, restless like a carp out of water. I looked
into his round glassy eyes and fed him bits of
algae and plankton. But he's shrinking. Anyone can
see. This morning he was a minnow. I didn't want to
come home one day to find him minuscule, molecular,
floating in a coffee cup above the mantle like
whale food. I had to set him free.

So I drove to the coast, with my father the
minnow in a fish bowl strapped into the passenger
seat, frolicking as the water sloshed from side to
side. From his erratic swimming I could tell he was
nervous about the imminent storm, and my driving on
slick roads. *"It's okay, Dad,"* I said, patting the
fish bowl as though it were his hand. He kept
worrying about what to cook for dinner, and whether
I would ever marry that boyfriend. I held my finger
to my lips to shush his worried flapping, and he
stopped circling the bowl, and I realized we both
knew we were headed somewhere strange.

I poured him lovingly into the ocean and
watched the water blend and stir. I stood there
hoping he would swim away into the depths; I waited
until the sky began to darken and the ocean became
the air became the ocean. Still, when I am near the
ocean, I hear my father whispering. *"Sweets,"* he
croons, *"The whole world is a fish bowl."* I pace
the edges of the ocean, forlorn, squinting at the
walls of the sky. I keep my door unlocked. I keep
my lights on. I know he isn't coming back, but if
he does, I want him to find his way. When the fog
sits on the house in the morning, I cry out for him
and hope he'll hear. But I know he can't hear me
underwater. I know that to him my voice is muted by
the ocean, and all he can hear are sea shanties
sinking towards the bottom.

Lies My Father Told Me:

1) *Stars,* he said, sitting in his own fog of cigarette smoke, *are a map for the rest of us.*

2) *Beauty,* he said, *is when the snow melts and then all the plants remember.*

3) *The disillusionment of adulthood,* he said, *is caused by drunken sailors still dreaming of tigers in red weather.*

4) *The lies we cling to come from lost tigers,* he claimed. So they prance through purple hours, casting shadows on peonies.

5) *Love,* he said, gnawing on his cigar, *is like catch-and-release. You have to let her go to preserve the resource.*

6) *Women,* he said. *All women are mermaids. They deny it. They dress up real nice and paint on their faces. But you should see them swim.*

7) *Your mother,* he admitted, *was half halibut. Hair the color of tilapia, mackerels in her eyes, she had a clam-shell for a heart. I was a fool for dreaming I could catch her.*

8) *Your mother painted her eyes peacock green and ruffled her cloak as she pranced to fish markets, holding back the saltwater in her eyes.*

9) *Sometimes,* he reminisced, *in good poetry she used a mollusk for a fan, and sunned herself on seashores from fairy tales.*

10) *So after your mother left, all the plants became tentacles. They tried to grab me, suction cups and crags, because they thought I was the sun.*

11) *That's why Judaism,* he said, pointing his nose to the clouds and smelling the sea, *is remembering all the women whose tears formed the ocean, and cherishing their sacrifices by following strict routines.*

12) He brushed the dirt from his anchor and mentally checked off the light switches in the house.

13) I could see he was agonizing, so I asked him, *Dad, which way is north?*

14) He snorted, a chortle, and held his pointer finger up to the weather, a skyscraper filled with clouds, and asked: *Do you smell that lingering dream? It's ripening like tilapia.*

15) *North is unavoidable,* he said. *Like Yiddish grandfathers and spilled milk.*

Heartbeat (a dream)

I fell in love with a grandfather clock. It was a gift from my father. It stood firmly in the corner, ticking away my childhood. I listened to it hum, groaning like a refrigerator without food. It was built like a tower, with a cloudy heart. Sometimes, at night, it turned into a sleeping lion, clicking its claws on the linoleum, growling at the rising sun. Even when I knew nothing, I knew the clock would keep counting, organizing my life into neat ticks and chimes. I wept for fear the clock would stop. In it, I saw my own face reflected, gazing out of the mechanism, feeling the walls, like a trapped prisoner. There is nothing like the gift of time bestowed on young women by their fathers. Even my dreams are pierced by logic and assertive sounds. But I loved my grandfather clock. Even after he was gone, I still heard him counting, adding the seconds and multiplying primes, trying to unlock the memories we took for granted. Even after he was gone, I heard him whispering algebra out the window to the weather, and waiting like an abacus for the snow to erase the world.

Dear Mathematician

The Mathematician's Wife

A Theorem (Woman)

Arithmetic drifted in her clouds. Newton chiseled
worry lines into her face, literature knitted her
hair, tangles of physics brushed freckled
shoulders. Her eyes, absolute zero. Green. A
matrix. I held her hand.

She unraveled, thread by silvery thread. Atoms
eroded from fingertips, exponents wallowed in
shadow. The residue of her numbers hovered,
investigating pretzel crumbs long forgotten.

A Hyperbola (Clock)

She made apples fall from trees. She shook Darwin's
sun. Fractions and exponents multiplied in crushed
footprints, forgotten. I calculated her. Strange 7s
perched in trees, 8s multiplied in the breeze; I
knew, the way you know about a melon.

I thought X would remain constant. I forgot to
factor Y (Years) and Z (memory).

A Ratio (Spiderweb)

The mathematics of daffodils. Her sun hat to
sundress; 3:1. Atoms still picked over pretzel
crumbs. I longed for the proper equation to explain
her back into the ivy.

X got forgetful. Forgot to take her medicine,
forgot to take her bath, forgot to wear her bra at
the grocery. X even forgot Y.

Symmetry (Evening)

Daffodils. Just me and the ivy, blowing and
growing, unraveling into entropy in a garden.

10 Variables (A Matrix)

1) I tried to paint my grandfather, and the figure devolved into flowers. He loved his garden. He was always gardening, until he couldn't.

2) Instead of him I think about my mother. It is easier to worry about her than to realize that even Grandpa's math couldn't save him.

3) I think about him when I teach. He would be so overwhelmed by a community college classroom. He preferred Madame Butterfly and potatoes when nobody was looking.

4) When my grandmother died, he took me on dates to all their special places. There was nothing left in his world. I held his hand and felt as though there was time between us.

5) When I was a child, he took me hiking in Yosemite. *"What's the square root of your address?"* he would ask, as we peered down Glacier Point and all the busy people looked like ants. I never knew the answer. Still, he kept asking.

6) It turned out the mathematician hated vegetables. Physics read like a comic book to him, but the logic of the food pyramid: sheer science fiction. He snuck cookies when my mother wasn't looking. Tell-tale crumbs lingered on his sweater vests.

7) When my grandmother was dying, he lay next to her for 4 days silently holding her hand.

8) He was a slob. After my grandmother died, he left underwear everywhere.

9) His derailed train of thought lay in steaming mechanical parts strewn about the garage, amidst the glinting recycling, overflowing with Diet Coke cans. The sun passed across the mess casting long-fingered shadows, which thumbed through yellowed newspapers, and waited for the door to open.

10) The train was very close to his house. I would swim in his pool and hear the train bells ringing. Low-flying planes would pass overhead. People were always transporting. Zaide would sit, legs crossed, leaning on his cane, dark glasses, head on a tilt, 90 years old, perched at a moment's notice to jump in and save me if I drowned.

Lies my Grandfather Told Me:

1) *The skyline is just a convergence of altitudes and redwoods. And my memory is speckled with calculus.*

2) *She was the alpha to my beta,* he said, *the gamma-ray to my heart.*

3) *Cars pass by like cosines,* he murmured, his thoughts competing with the sounds of traffic.

4) "*Mathematics is where reason resides.* He paused, looked me over, then said: *After your grandmother died, I was merely a placeholder for quantities.*"

5) *Your grandmother filled the perimeters of my living room with ballads about young tragic lovers. She made math into music.*

6) He looked down at his plate, and dropped his fork, and said: *at night, I still feel her volume, strumming against the mattress with metronomic precision.*

7) *I know that I am just a placeholder for your Yiddish grandfather*, he said, eating potatoes in a kitchen with a ticking clock.

8) *Memory,* he said, *is batting the exponents from your bookshelves, and napping regularly as an excuse to dream about the wilderness behind your eyes.*

Moments when the trajectory of my life suddenly became clear:

1) In preschool, my teacher set up chairs and told us we were flying to Hawaii. Each of us received a shiny golden American Airlines button. I cherished that button. We sat in orderly lines, as Mrs. Darby made plane noises with her mouth. *Vroom, vroom*, she said, and all the buildings got smaller. *Chug, chug*, she said, a little turbulence over Mexico. I looked out the imaginary window and saw the Pacific frothing with life. When the plane jerked to a halt, and a plastic lei was placed around my neck, another, more tangible lei was wrapped around my life. As I sipped imaginary coconut milk and listened to hula music, I felt sunshine, real sunshine. I felt strange, I felt wild, but mostly, I felt far away.

2) In college, I fell in love with poetry, so I wrote a thesis for the esteemed Wendy's franchise poet, Joe Wenderoth. Joe cherished John Berryman, had a scraggly beard, and a habit of drinking Diet Rite soda. (And whiskey on weeknights.) He played a soft-core porn for students at his house, a movie of a man making love to a motorcycle while his wife lay asleep in the next room, dreaming of roses and the aurora borealis. *"This,"* proclaimed Joe, picking lint from under his fingernail, *"is art."* I wondered whether Joe might get fired. But I watched the naked man's body jive and thrust to the music, and I pretended to understand.

3) When I became a teacher, I marched into my classroom, armed only with philosophy and poetry, and asked the students what they thought of Aristotle. Blank stares searched windows for ticking clocks and passing trains. The whole city, in one small classroom, was mourning gun violence,

and I could hear the breathlessness echoing between
myself and the chalkboard. *"Who knows what a
pronoun is?"* I asked, knowing I had lost a part of
myself on that battlefield of desks and flickering
smartphones, but still, I pushed on, head bent to
the wind, hell-bent on looking competent.

Forget-Me-Not (Lillies)

Anxieties darted through my head as I prepared to fly to my childhood home. I had so much to finish first. Pay the red light ticket, buy that damn city sticker, call Chicago Memorial about that bill. Something caught my eye. A fluttering. I was approaching the Irving Park El stop, when the train rolled over sounding like a waterfall, and then paused. But that wasn't the flutter. Nor was it the slight breeze filtering through the hallways between the buildings, easing the moisture on my skin. It was humid. God it was humid. I was sweating and my blood too, was fluttering from the heat. It made me think of my father, his heart pausing at red lights on an operating table in the San Francisco fog.

The flutter came from a dark bar behind the bus stop. It was named after a ship named after a woman, and the whole place was sleeping--chairs were stacked on tables, empty glasses winked and dreamt back through the window. I squinted through my own reflection in the darkness. A pulse. A beat. A trapped butterfly tapped back at me through the glass. It was a monarch. Its wings looked like prowling tigers. It pounded its insect body against the dark glass, again and again, in a panic. I thought for a moment of Virginia Woolf watching a moth die, a mild sentiment coursing through her elegant fingers tapping the typewriter. I was compelled to save it. But, I knew I would miss my train, which would make me miss my flight, which would make me miss my home. And I knew I couldn't save it. I knew it would die. So I pressed on.

Later, in California, on a different train, heading to that same childhood home, I gazed out the panoramic window. Near my grandfather's old house, I saw a sign with blue, cupped hands. It read, *"Choose hope,"* and the number for a hotline. I had forgotten. There was an epidemic of teenage suicides on those tracks in Palo Alto. For years, depressed upper-middle-class Silicon Valley teenagers had flung their bodies against honking horns and sheet metal, pat, pat, patting against the dark glass, questing for something, anything else, as their lives (or lack of lives) flashed before their eyes. Maybe in those final moments, they finally answered a riddle, or calculated a square root, or maybe, just maybe, they visualized Virginia Woolf, wading into the water, rocks heavy against her thighs, as the cold consumed the poetry.

Memory is a strange father. It's funny how you tend to remember sweetly: the lazy afternoons skipping rocks, the alpine glow in the mountains. It's easy to move away from a town and forget the epidemic of children committing suicide. It's easy to leave Chicago behind, and ignore the classroom voices, and the white lilies on the news, when I close my eyes. It's tempting to forget the last days, when my grandfather looked past me, out windows at a world he could no longer see, and spoke of operas where even though he loves her, she dies.

Dear Musician

A Cavatina (No Rain)

Tormented, the musician forgot (blamed) music. He cursed clacking heels, and sonorous chirping humans.

Consequently, he spent days in dark rooms, and grew a beard. This beard was no fisherman's beard, but it was scraggly, and nice.

He used his piano as a bookshelf. He threw his drumsticks out the window and they spun like rain.

"Music, let me alone," he cursed. But still, he heard Haydn when he drove in and out of tunnels. There was that horrid rhythm when he chewed his eggs.

He wanted to make music disappear. To gather up all cantatas, carols, and cavatinas, and hit pause, so he would not be bothered. Then, he presumed, he could live.

He plucked all the chords and the refrains from breezes, and etudes from sleeping cities. Arpeggios came from sputtering cars, clefs and codas from honking seagulls. He shook all the music and he trapped it on a yellow train.

The train supped and sang. It emitted strange glows. The train did not know it was full of music, but then, most musical instruments don't know either.

The fisherman in his drifting boat, heard the yellow train, and thought of something that wasn't fish.

The mathematician in his blowing garden, did not hear the yellow train because his ears were as old as the fisherman's sea.

The musician heard the yellow train, and said, "Christ, what have I done?" But by then all the

music had already gone to wherever it is that
trains go when we can no longer see.

The musician scratched at his beard, and listened.
There was no sound. He got up, quiet, quiet, and
walked quietly to look.

In clouds, silent whales.

Bellowing, the musician tossed his heart, a
harpoon, out the window.

A Cantata (Rain)

The musician found a harp and mistook it for a heart. He strummed it in order to keep a pulse. He mistook rhythm for circulation. He displaced sounds and birthed breath.

But he was making sound in time to express emotions and ideas through significant forms and elements of harmony.

All around him: harmony. Trees swayed, and birds perched, and the sun moved slowly across the sky.

When the musician discovered that he had been making music all along, he was disgusted. The music reminded him of bars named after ships named after women.

He vowed not to sleep until the music stopped. He waited years.

A very old mathematician watered a daffodil. Where he walked trailed numbers.

In that strange year, the trees were made of cardboard. The musician scratched at a bite on his arm, sandpaper. He began to question atoms as he watched them flit like fleas.

Rain. An aria. No need for music.

The musician went home.

But in that sandpaper year, the musician had no home. Only a harp that was not a heart. Pumping, pumping, strings that refused to fall from clouds.

10 Uses for Music

1. To ward off hungry pigeons.

2. To thaw digits by fake fire.

3. To invent allowances for deep dish pizza consumption.

4. To press silver dollars into the blooming hands of street performers dressed in gold.

5. To place rubies on the air, cautiously, like Christmas lights, but more tragic.

6. To cast his fisherman's line through the cold front, questing for wilderness despite rush-hour traffic.

7. Because he wanders and wonders beneath the El tracks, confusing sparks for sun rays.

8. Since his voice illuminates the night like lightning bugs confusing their own bodies with stars.

9. Perhaps his positive vibes can change the world, one hungry pigeon at a time.

10. Because he knows no other way to ward off the bears who haunt him, so he holds your hand.

A Beginning (An Ending)

That summer he was working on his opus
and he locked himself away in the nocturne,
I heard murmurs and echoes of vibrato
percolating through the floor boards.

He looked a bit like a deer in the rain,
a nervous listener,
long-necked,
an orchestra of antlers,
tuning in the forest.

The trees hummed in the key of "C,"
and he recited his requiem,
with tombstones in his eyes.
De Capo he said,
meant it wasn't over.

The birds played strange violins,
a string quartet to lull the morning.
I waltzed down the scale towards
the Cheshire Cat
and begged him to serenade me to sleep.

About the Author

Originally from Los Altos, California, Rachel Slotnick is a painter and writer. She received her MFA from the School of the Art Institute of Chicago in May 2010. Her work is on permanent display at the Joan Flasch Artist Book Collection at the School of the Art Institute of Chicago. She is a sponsored muralist for the 35th, 46th and 47th wards, and her paintings are currently on display in a solo exhibition at Beauty & Brawn Art Gallery & Think Space. She was recently a finalist in the Gwendolyn Brooks Open Mic Awards. Look for her upcoming publications in Mad Hatter's Review, Thrice Fiction, and Tortoise Books. Rachel currently resides in Chicago where she works as Adjunct Faculty in Art Studio and English at Malcolm X College, and the Illinois Art Institute.

See the full scope of her work
at: www.rachelslotnick.com

About Tortoise Books

Slow and steady wins in the end, but the book industry often focuses on the fast-seller. Tortoise Books is dedicated to finding and promoting quality authors who haven't yet found a niche in the marketplace—writers producing memorable and engaging works that will stand the test of time.

Learn more at: www.tortoisebooks.com

www.ingramcontent.com/pod-product-compliance
Lightning Source LLC
Chambersburg PA
CBHW020439030426
42337CB00014B/1326